HERC
AND THE OLYMPIANS
A QUESTION AND ANSWER BOOK

by Susan Blackaby
illustrated by Mark Sparacio

inchworm
PRESS
™

Q: Where did the gods and goddesses of ancient Greece live?

A: Mount Olympus was home to the gods and goddesses. They were known as Olympians. Hades was the only god who didn't live there. He lived in the Underworld and did not often visit above ground.

Q: How did the gods and goddesses spend their time?

A: The gods and goddesses had a peaceful life on Mount Olympus, but because they lived forever, they were often bored and crabby. To pass the time, they meddled in the lives of mortals on the earth.

Q: Zeus was king of Mount Olympus. What were his main duties?

A: Zeus was the most powerful Olympian. He decided when the sun would rise and set. He controlled the change of seasons and stirred up bad weather.

Q: How did Zeus feel about humans?

A: Zeus was very fond of humans, and he tried to help them when he could. He was gentle with them because he knew they were weak. When he did lose his temper, he hurled thunderbolts down on the earth. He was tough, but he was also fair.

Q: Who was Zeus' queen?

A: Hera was the most powerful goddess on Mount Olympus and ruled with Zeus. She was worshipped as the protector of marriage and women.

Q: What made Hera angry, and what happened when she got mad?

A: Hera was jealous of Zeus' affection for mortals. When she got mad, she got even. Like the other Olympians, meddling in people's lives was one of her favorite pastimes. For example, Hera hounded Zeus' son Hercules for years before she finally left him alone.

Q: What were the twelve labors of Hercules?

A: **1.** He killed the Nemean lion.

2. He killed the Hydra.

3. He captured the golden-horned deer sacred to the goddess of the hunt, Artemis.

He snared the wild boar that terrorized the hill people.

5. He cleaned the stables of King Augeus.

6. He rid the forest lake of flesh-eating birds of p

7. He captured the mad, fire-breathing bull of Crete.

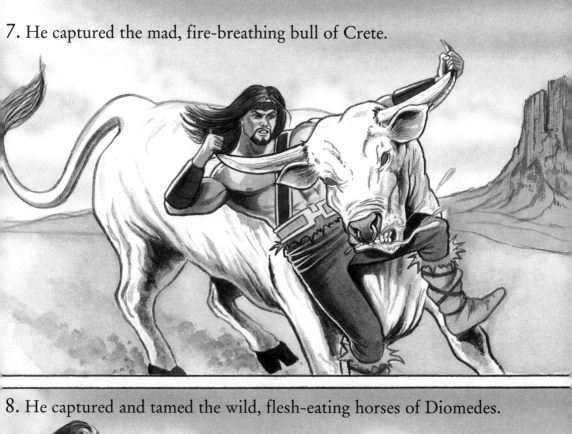

8. He captured and tamed the wild, flesh-eating horses of Diomedes.

9. He stole the belt of the Amazon queen, Hippolyte.

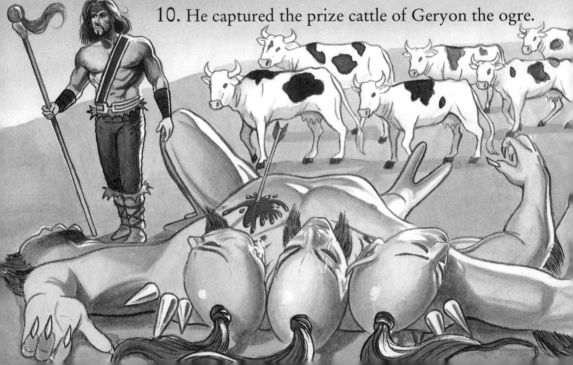

10. He captured the prize cattle of Geryon the ogre.

11. He took three golden apples from Hera's sacred tree.

12. He captured Cerberus, the guard dog of the Underworld.

Q: Which giant had the weight of the world on his shoulders?

A: The Titan Atlas was charged with holding up the sky. Hercules traded places with Atlas so that the giant could pick the golden apples for him. Atlas planned to double-cross Hercules and leave him to hold up the sky, but Hercules tricked him into taking it back.

Q: **Which god could be found hard at work under a volcano?**

A: The blacksmith god, Hephaestus, of course! He was the god of the forge. He made the special rattle that Athena gave to Hercules so that he could scare the flesh-eating birds and shoot them out of the sky for his sixth labor.

Q: How did Hades dress when he traveled from the Underworld?

A: Hades, the god of the Underworld, wore a magic helmet that made him invisible so that he could travel to the land of the living without being seen. Few who saw Hades in the Underworld ever returned to the land of the living. Persephone, Hades' wife, was allowed to leave only once each year.

Q: Which god worked as a messenger?

A: Hermes delivered messages for Zeus. His winged sandals made him fast on his feet. Hermes also led the dead to King Hades in the Underworld. Hermes guided Hercules to the three-headed dog, Cerberus, that guarded the gates to the Underworld.

Q: **Which goddess was formed from the forehead of Zeus?**

A: Athena. She was born full grown, dressed in a suit of golden armor. She was the goddess of wisdom, war, technical skills, crafts, and the city. Athens, the capital of Greece, was named for her. She gave Hercules the sacred rattle that he used to complete his sixth labor.

Zeus
king of the gods

Poseidon
god of the oceans

Hades
*god of the Underworld
and wealth*

Hera
queen of the gods

Hestia
goddess of the hearth

Ares
god of war

Athena
*goddess of wisdom,
war, and crafts*

Apollo
god of light and truth

Aphrodite
goddess of love and beauty

Hermes
*god of motion, sleep, and
dreams*

Artemis
*goddess of the moon,
hunting, and children*

Hephaestus
god of the forge